Live Your Worth

How to maximize your value and optimize your
greatness in every area of your life

Daniela Jean

Printed in the United States of America

ISBN 978-0692955352

All scripture quotations are taken from the *Holy Bible, New International Version*®, **NIV**®· Copyright © 1973, 1978, 1984, 2011 by Biblica, Inc. ® Used by permission. All rights reserved worldwide. AMPC, ESV, NKJV, NLT

Cover design by: Vessel Design

September 2017

Straighten up your crown
Don't look down
No need to wear a frown
You are upward bound

-Daniela

ACKNOWLEDGEMENTS

Mom & Dad thank you for all your hard
work and dedication.
Shirline, my dear sister thanks for always
being a sounding board of truth.
Love you

DEDICATION
This book is dedicated
to ALL the underdogs.
You are more than WORTH IT!

CONTENTS

INTRODUCTION

I have come to the realization that discovering myself and knowing my worth are the prerequisites to living a purposeful life. The more I come to understand my unique traits and qualities, the more I am able to conquer the world. This coupled with establishing my own set of core values and personal convictions have catapulted me into the next level of greatness. The truth is that we all have the potential to achieve greatness; it is in all of us. Once you realize this, the less you will compromise your values and the more you will optimize golden opportunities. Your potential will be realized. Your knowledge utilized. Your faith exercised. Your dreams actualized. The possibilities of what you can accomplish are endless when you realize that you already have all it takes to be great. Greatness in your unique area of expertise. Greatness in your character. Greatness in decision-making. Greatness in your lane of life. Greatness is attainable. The upgrade is at your fingertips. You can experience it simply by walking in the knowledge that you are wonderfully made, you are royalty and you were created to be: Blessed. You are called to greater. You are loved. You are all these things and more. It's not a hype, it's a fact. So now is the time to live and to realize your purpose, passions and potential every single day.

Let us embark on this journey together.

LET US LIVE OUR WORTH OUT LOUD!

-Daniela

1

LOVE YOURSELF ENOUGH

I remember a time when I depended so much on the acknowledgment and affirmation of others. Waiting on the approval of others to feel valued and loved. I would fish for compliments and pats on the back. Sometimes even feeling totally dejected if no one acknowledged my "awesomeness". After years of pity parties, I had to face the facts. I was worth it and I needed to start acting like it. I had to dig deep and determine that my value wasn't dependent on someone's assessment of me. Loving, accepting, and discovering my true self opened the floodgates to an awesome opportunity. The opportunity to truly love myself unconditionally. I finally acknowledged that I was made in the amazing image of my Creator. That was all the affirmation I needed. The journey to loving myself had official began.

How deep is your love for yourself?

I am not talking about that self-absorbed, self-centered stuff. Nor am I referring to that superficial fluffy stuff. No. I'm talking about that deep acceptance of the person you are. The person that the Creator has uniquely crafted in His image. Caring for yourself intently with gentleness and consistency. Do you love yourself enough? Enough to actualize your potential. Enough to live out your dreams. Enough to eliminate negative influences. Enough to fight for your future.

Enough to Live Your Worth.

Self-love starts with understanding the value you possess within. Your life is worth more than you know. You are Priceless. Paid for by the ultimate act of love. #John3:16

Healing

Accepting your features, flaws and failures is part of loving yourself. But beyond what your eyes see, your soul also speaks. Do the broken parts of your life limit your ability to fully love yourself? The fragments of your life need to mend so that you can bloom. You will need courage during this healing process. Courage to forgive past hurts. Courage to get therapy, counseling or to seek spiritual counsel. Courage to let your soul finally heal. Healing the soul allows for self-love to freely govern every aspect of your life. When love finally shines through, it will illuminate your worth.

R-E-S-P-E-C-T

Self-love and self-respect work hand in hand. The more you uphold your standards, morals and personal convictions, the more self-respect you'll develop. The more you know and understand the inner workings of your heart and mind, and identify your core values, the more you will respect and love yourself. Discovering what makes you unique adds value and freedom to your life. The elements that you bring to the table of life should be valued, loved and respected.

The Love Tank

You have an endless supply of love and its roots run deep. This love is not dependent on your looks, your negative opinions or your short comings. According to 1 John 4:19, We love because He first loved us. BOOM! God's love for us gives us the ability to love ourselves and others freely. Mark 12:31 instructs us to "Love your neighbor as yourself". This also hints that we must love and respect ourselves to be able to reciprocate it to others. Self-love is a prerequisite. Attempting to love someone else without fully loving yourself is a risky task. It's like driving on an empty tank of gas. You won't make it far, before you need to fill up. Fill up on that John 3:16 Love. That 1 Corinthians 13 Love. That Romans 8:31-37 Love.

Walk It Out

Embody who you truly are. Walk in the realization that you are enough just as you are. You've got this! Accept, nurture and respect yourself and positivity will follow. Some introspection is needed in order for this to sink in. Take a closer look within. You may have to uninstall self-hatred and download self-acceptance. You may have to uninstall self-doubt and download self-affirmation. Appreciate your attributes and see yourself as a masterpiece. Learn to compliment yourself. Don't put yourself down. Your self-talk shapes how you see yourself. So speak positively and with confidence. Everything about you may not be perfect, but like a masterpiece you are precious and breathtaking in the eye of the Artist.

"For we are God's masterpiece.
He has created us anew in Christ Jesus,
so we can do the good things
he planned for us long ago"
Ephesians 2:10, NLT.

Learning to love every inch of yourself unconditionally is vital. Appreciate how far you've come and enjoy the journey of your progress. Accept that each phase of life is a stepping stone to fulfilling your purpose. As you enjoy the journey to complete self-love, your love will spill over and saturate people around you.

It's Within!

All you need to thrive is already inside of you; you simply need to activate it. Write down your dreams and innermost desires. Visualize yourself achieving them. Sometimes life's harsh realities tarnish our outlook and sabotage our future endeavors. The love you have inside can die if it is never released. Or worse yet, it can turn into bitterness. Through self-love, you will discover what comes naturally to you. When you love yourself, you also give the world the opportunity to fall in love with you.

Discovering your strengths and weaknesses isn't an easy process, but this process creates growth. Loving yourself is much easier when you remember that God loved you first! You were made in His image. Though you see yourself as flawed, you are His masterpiece.

If someone didn't compliment me or invite me to a dinner party, I would feel unworthy. When I was overlooked and undermined, I felt less love for myself. I doubted myself and my purpose because others didn't acknowledge me. We must never allow another human to validate or affirm our self-love. This can be a

dangerous game. The love you have for yourself shouldn't be validated by the opinion of others. You must not affirm your self-love through someone else's opinion. I finally had an epiphany and I realized that I am because God says that I am. I am a conqueror. I am royalty. I am a child of the KING. No one can take that away from me. People around you will get the memo of your status change once you believe and accept it. I love and accept my quirkiness and creativity. What do you love and accept about yourself? If you can't be fully comfortable with yourself, how in the world can people be comfortable with you or around you? You are a gift to the world. Sometimes, loving others is so much easier than accepting ourselves. No matter what others perceive or assume about you. Love yourself!
You were created in love, by a God of love through love. Now that's a whole lot of love! Remember John 3:16. The love that you were created in supersedes any self-hate. You must be able to visualize and actualize the endless possibilities in your life. These possibilities will become a reality through self-love and personal growth. Learn to love your life with the trials and triumphs that come your way. You are the CEO of your life! Embrace it and take ownership.

Loving yourself will prompt you to want to fix and focus on the cracks in your life. Consequently, when people come into your life they won't be overwhelmed by your insecurities. Be brave. Love yourself enough to tidy up inside and out. Appreciate the good, uproot the bad and discover the treasures that lie within you. Our worth speaks volume when we let it shine. Let go of everything in your life that may have negative side effects on your self-worth. Uproot the polluted roots in your life. Let the process begin today. Some examples of negative roots may include:

- Bad company
- Negative self-talk
- Haters and naysayers
- Procrastination

We must value ourselves so much that others will have no choice but to follow suit. Typically, the way in which we allow others to treat us is an indication of how much, or how little, we love and value ourselves. It's only when something is valued that it is deemed valuable. You are a valuable gift. Think highly of yourself. Learn to understand your complexities and accentuate your best characteristics. Assess yourself from head to toe. Inside and out. Write down your observations. What are your highlights? What are your areas of insecurities? Make note of them, then pray for guidance and seek out a mentor, a life coach or a spiritual leader who can help you formulate a plan to improve your life.

The world sees you through the lenses you provide. Don't let those lenses be cloudy or dirty, because you are unsure of yourself. Wear who you are as a badge of honor and not a mere happenstance. You are not a fluke of nature. Remember that you were fashioned with purpose and love. Intentionally made to carry out a unique purpose.

Self-love will attract love. When looking for love, look up to God and look within. Everything else is a bonus. The ones who are meant to love you will love you more when you learn to love yourself. Love is a magnet. If your own personal force is weak what will you attract? Self-love generates an attraction that is powerful and undeniable. Love brings comfort, ease and familiarity. The old adage that honey brings more bees than vinegar is tried and true. Love attracts love.

We all need a shoulder to lean on from time to time. It's good to have a listening ear or a confidant to pour our hearts to. Yet the ability to stand on one's two feet is paramount. Relying on others for our sanity or purpose is too large of an expectation to place on mere mortals. We should love people and love ourselves enough to trust our intuition and inner compass. Love yourself, it is the key to survival.

Things I love about myself

1 _____
2 _____
3 _____
4 _____
5 _____
6 _____
7 _____
8 _____
9 _____
10 _____

Things I would like
to improve about myself

1_____

I can start by:_____

2_____

I can start by:_____

3_____

I can start by:_____

15 Ways to Enjoy Life More

1. Schedule time for you
2. Treat yourself to healthy food
3. Let go of your worries
4. Enjoy your friends and family more
5. Pamper yourself
6. Unplug electronics devices and plug into nature
7. Set aside 15 minutes of quiet time daily
8. Go after your dreams
9. Let your creativity soar
10. Take care of your money: Invest and save
11. Read lots of books
12. Take care of your spirit, body and mind
13. Work for God
14. Donate to charity or volunteer
15. Look in the mirror and smile

❧Share your Thoughts❧

2

GO WITH THE FLOW

I grew up in a very strict household. There were lots of rules and lots of restrictions. This really caused me to stay in my shell and to become quite hesitant. In later years, it became so hard for me to make decisions and to stand on my own. Making big decisions was horrifying for me. I had a very restricted mindset and I didn't know how to react or express myself. Everything seemed like a roadblock or obstacle that was too high for me to surpass. It wasn't until I rediscovered my worth and freedom in Christ, that I began to seize opportunities and to walk into my destiny. I learned to go with the flow and to walk in the Spirit. I was never steered wrong as long as I learned to listen and obey to the Spirit's guidance. There were so many opportunities that I was so afraid to grab because I had been held back for so long. The shackles of hesitancy no longer weigh me down. I claim John 8:36 "So if the Son sets you free, you will be free indeed."

Life is a journey and we are all making our way through it. There are detours along the way, yield signs and speed bumps that make the road quite interesting. Red lights, green lights, hitchhikers and pit stops. This journey called life is extremely strenuous and calls for a high level of endurance. So when we get to a crossroad it's often difficult to know exactly which path to take or follow. Many times, that particular road, be it a job offer or relationship, may seem like the perfect route, "that golden opportunity", the greatest option, yet we are unsure. We know our worth. We love ourselves. We know our unique gifts but we doubt the actuality of our greatness. We psych ourselves out of an opportunity for many reasons. Sometimes we don't believe we deserve it, and other times we believe a better opportunity may come. Throughout this journey, we must understand that hesitation can lead to missed opportunities. Each opportunity or chance has a shelf life. We can't allow them to expire. Sometimes all we have is a nanosecond to make a life altering decision. So remember that no action, delayed reaction or miscommunication can all lead to deviated destinies.

"Go with the flow," is a phrase that you have heard many times before. Our life's journey will take us through a series of waves. Some high, some low, some smooth, others tumultuous, nevertheless we must go with the flow of life. We have to ride the waves like seasoned pros. One way to do this is by equipping ourselves for the journey. The right gear is essential. Be it by continuing your education or by building a strong support network, we must surround ourselves with elements that will ensure our success. When we equip ourselves and snatch all the opportunities within our reach, we develop a hunger to win. Don't psyche yourself out. You deserve the blessings and victories that come your way. Often times, we are afraid of the strong currents and we are intimidated by the high tides on our journey. Ride the wave and you will come out victorious.

Walk boldly into your destiny. Do not fear the unknown but instead, hold on to faith. The road of life can lead us to various avenues of opportunity. Often times making the right choice can seem difficult and daunting. Be bold and confident. Rely on faith to divinely steer you. Don't rely solely on the advice of others. Pray and seek the will of God. Trust divine guidance and believe that all things are working for your good. People will not always understand the decisions you make. This should not stop you for living out your purpose. Be wise and aware of pitfalls and hazards along your way. They may come in the form of haters, naysayers and spectators. Nevertheless, go with the flow, you are making strides.

Be alert. There will be warning signs along the way that you must take heed to. Sharks and lurkers will often be placed in strategic spots to bring you down, so rely on divine maneuvering to help you steer clear of these dangers. Other times we may become haughty and as a result our vision becomes cloudy. We start seeing mirages that are only full of false potential. Before you act grand, seek God's plan. Every road is not meant to be ventured! Trust your instincts, pray for guidance and walk by faith. Going with the flow is essentially walking by faith. Proverbs 16:3 reminds us to "Commit to the LORD whatever you do, and he will establish your plans." It's a well-balanced concept that cannot be denied or ignored. Going with the flow is knowing when to pump the breaks and when to accelerate. It's assessing your situation and understanding which course of action will take you to the next level. The journey of life involves many decisions, some of which must be made at a moment's notice. You can miss the opportunity to venture to the next level if you don't live in the present. The ability to recognize opportunities that align with your purpose is paramount. Let's not forget that many situations may involve the process of being patient and making calculated decisions. This flow of life may not always be rapid and swift. Haste often makes waste. It may take more time than expected as you fully analyze the flow of a situation. It may take months or a few weeks, as you assess the flow of things and or people. I used to think that going with the flow meant being blind to the darts of life with an air of naivety. On the contrary, going with the flow involves being wise, intuitive and brave. Be constantly ready by working on your craft, deepening relationships and industry contacts. Don't obsess over timelines and deadlines. Obsessing will only block your flow. Being obsessed negates all principles of going with the flow. Let your faith conquer your fears and anxiety. Obsessing is futile. Worrying or over-analyzing won't change any situation. Stay positive and relinquish your worries. Trust the process. Put God first in all you do. Go with the flow of His divine leading. Follow your internal compass. No self-doubt or hesitancy. Only focus and determination.

When things follow their natural progression, the results are always organic. So allow things to flow toward you. Don't be a stick in the mud, let things flow to you. And when the flow doesn't feel right, don't be afraid to pause and find higher ground.

You will come to a point when everything lines up and the moment is right, don't fear the unknown. Don't sabotage yourself with doubt and indecisiveness. Go with the right flow and keep your moral high. We can't force the hand of life but we can play the cards we've been dealt and use our deck to our advantage.

FLOW through life with wisdom and divine precision!

❧ Share your Thoughts ❦

3

GREATER

Greatness is within me!

We all have expectations; the belief that something will happen. It's a normal human phenomenon for us to hope and anticipate certain things. Though we have good intentions, sometimes our expectations are far-fetched and unrealistic. This can be true especially as it relates to the people in our lives. We want them to always be on time, keep their word, love us, read our thoughts and keep us happy. These expectations are not unreasonable to anticipate from those we love, but frankly, we need to expect more of ourselves and a tad bit less of people as it relates to our goals and contentment. This doesn't mean that we should let people off the hook and discard all of our standards, but we only open ourselves to disappointment and frustration if we expect perfection from imperfect beings. We should rightfully set healthy boundaries and objectives for people in our life. However, we need to set realistic expectations for ourselves and follow through with our own aspirations and dreams. What goals have you set years ago that still haven't been fulfilled? People may forget or neglect us, but we have a greater responsibility to ourselves. We deserve to keep promises we've made to ourselves and see them through. You can strive to change, but you really can't force someone else to change. Never forget how much power you have within. 1 John 4:4 declares that "greater is He who is in you than he who is in the world."

Everything you need to become the best version of yourself is already inside of you. You have the power within you to succeed, so you owe it to yourself to stay motivated. And as you motivate yourself, you will be able to motivate others. The greatness inside of you will empower others to push harder. We can make great adjustments to our health, our spiritual life and so much more if we make the effort. This is not an easy task, but it's one worth trying.

Our character and work ethic can greatly influence change in the people we encounter. We must convert our power of influence to fuel the change within ourselves first then in others. The key is to keep pushing. We must know and understand that though we are imperfect, we can still strive for greatness. Though we may fall or fail, we are still winners. The goals that we have set for ourselves are still attainable. The real work comes into play when we acknowledge the greatness within us and tap into that power. A "bad" day or "bad" year doesn't dictate the outcome of our destinies. We must expect what is great. For we ourselves are GREAT!

"I can do all things through Christ who gives me strength" Philippians 4:13, NLT

We ultimately must put all our aspirations and expectations in God. He can't fail. He doesn't lie. And in Him, we find our identity of greatness.

"Then God said, 'Let us make man in our image, in our likeness' " Genesis 1:26.

When you believe in God earnestly and totally, then you will have the power to believe in yourself. He created you. He won't steer you wrong and He is always on time. When it comes to God, there is power in your level of expectation. His promises are true.

"You will always be at the top, never at the bottom" Deuteronomy 28:13.

He is faithful and will always step into the gap to fill our needs and shortcomings. Often time it's hard to trust people. It's actually hard to trust ourselves sometimes. But what a relief that we can trust God 100% of the time! Through God, we receive the power to change and the wisdom to understand that we can't change others.

We all have different journeys to follow and we all travel at different speeds. Therefore, we should simply focus on our pace and our unique path. Timing is everything. We must be patient with people. Knowing when to stay and when to walk away. Be the change you want to see. Raise up the level of expectations in your own life and watch your environment change. Expect more of yourself. Pray for those you anticipate change from. People decide to make the right changes when they are ready to, don't force it. Ultimately, if that person genuinely wants to be in your life, they will make the right changes and meet your expectations.

At the end of the day, we must be the change we want to see. We must push ourselves. We must expect greatness from our lives. Be willing to get out of your comfort zone. Step outside of the box. Stop relying on people to fulfill your life with their greatness. Be good to yourself and encourage yourself. Trust God and trust His timing. Put your faith in Him. There is power in your level of expectation.

❧ Share your Thoughts ❧

_____

_____

_____

_____

_____

_____

_____

_____

_____

_____

_____

_____

_____

_____

_____

_____

_____

_____

_____

_____

_____

_____

_____

_____

_____

4

SAME HABITS = SAME RESULTS

Comfort is important. We all have that comfy sweater with the hole in the elbow, or those baggy sweatpants with the missing drawstring. We enjoy being comfortable. And this comfort extends to so much more than our clothes. We are creatures of habit and we get comfortable with our daily routines as well. Our habits become so second nature to us that they become embedded in the fabric of our character. Some of these habits are good. Like flossing and drinking lots of water. But some habits like overeating and lying can be detrimental to the course of our lives. Evaluate your daily habits and see which ones are leading you to sketchy behaviors. We must develop habits or routines that elevate our standards. Like I mentioned before, we are gifts to the world. We generally have to develop better habits to optimize our lives. In the next 24 hour period I challenge you to jot down your daily routine. From the minute you open your eyes to your bedtime prep, we must start developing habits that will uplift our mind, body and soul.

Upon analyzing my daily routine here is what I found: *Pressing the snooze button, which leads me to being late for work. Forgetting to pray. Skipping morning devotional. Not drinking enough water. Skipping breakfast and grabbing a donut. Skipping the salad and opting for the fries. Fussing at coworkers/boss under my breath. Choosing to watch TV instead of doing nightly reading. Going out with my friends instead of finishing up assignments. Forgetting to do my nightly facial routine. No night time prayer.*

You get my point. I observed myself making these little choices daily and they became full blown habits. Embedded in my thought pattern and attitude, the slow soul decay had begun. Now you may think that these are harmless actions that can be easily rectified, and you are right, but think of the hundreds of habits that can eventually become life-threatening and may lead to illness, depression and isolation. Our habits affect our interpersonal relationships and this is why we have to address them. Loving yourself includes reversing certain habits into productive practices. We must understanding that everything we choose to do has a negative or positive effect. So take a moment to reassess your habits.

Create a chart like the one below and counter your bad habits with positive alternatives. Here's mine. I grouped some habits together and found awesome solutions:

Bad Habits	New Adjustments/Alternatives
*Being late for work. *Forgetting to pray *Skipping morning devotional	~Go to sleep earlier ~Set 2 alarms with reminder ~Get A.M. Prayer Partner
*Not drinking enough water	~Have Water Bottle near keys from night before
*Skipping breakfast *Skipping the salad and opting for the fries	~ Grocery shopping on Sunday (set time) ~Make meal list/ Meal Prep
*Bad-mouthing coworkers/boss under my breath	~Memorize and practice fruits of the spirit-recite them when I get mad ~Read Galatians 5:22-23 daily
*Watching useless TV	~Decide which shows uplift my spirit and set alarm for devotional
*Going out with my friends instead of doing school work	~Chat with friends about my new priorities and set monthly night out
*Skipping skin care routine	~Set alarm for night routine

Now that you see what I'm working on, create your own list and find an accountability partner. Remember that the greatest project you can work on is yourself. Progress and success begin when our habits reflects our goals. Your consistency is connected to your progress, so adjust your habits. If you believe that your daily routine is fool-proof, take a moment to pray for revelation and guidance. God can reveal any blind spots that maybe looming.

Our habits also relate to what behaviors we accept from others. Since relationships are an integral part of the human experience, we must have guidelines on what we accept and decline. We should all accept compliments and kudos but we must reject venom and malice. No human being should be subjected to being treated like a doormat or afterthought. There was a time when I accepted insults and backhanded compliments from people. I never spoke up and those comments slowly crept into my subconscious. I also believed what was said about me. In turn, my personal habits became a result of how people habitually treated me. I began to engage in self-destructive behavior based on what others said. All of this was subconscious, I didn't realize that I had allowed people's words and actions to influence my persona. No more allowing people to invade our lives with negative vibes and destructive actions! This is a bad practice. Since our environment plays a huge part in our lives, we must make it a habit to assess potential negativity. People's negative habits and abusive treatment can greatly influence our daily routines. We must love ourselves enough to know that we deserve more. We all deserve better and must dig deep for the courage to expect and demand it. God loves you. He daily provides for us and He calls us His children. We are royalty. Children of THE KING. Therefore, we have to uphold that standard in our dealings with others. Disrespect is not a habit we should allow people to practice on us, PERIOD. This also includes and is not limited to: belittlement, verbal abuse, physical abuse, sexual abuse, being ignored, used, bullied, cheated on and manipulated. We need to be discerning and use our intuition. We must pray, trust, and believe that we can be delivered from any situation. Some serious soul-searching is in order when we are determining which people truly need to be in our lives. Distance yourself from people who lead you towards a lifestyle of destruction. Do you have a bad habit of allowing people to treat you like a second-class citizen? Are people constantly making you feel worthless? Do people constantly make fun of you? Do they make you feel guilty? Have you accepted these behaviors as norms? Today is the day to set yourself free. You don't deserve it. You were created to live your best life. Life is a faith walk. Just move one foot at a time, make the changes that need to be made, one at a time and you will see progress.

It all starts with a decision to refuse to accept behaviors and habits that are the opposite of your identity in Christ. You are royalty. Keep your head up. Don't let your crown slip. Being royalty simple means that you should be treated with love and respect. While we all have different definitions of what love and respect mean, I can tell you that love and respect doesn't include a man or woman putting their hands on you. It doesn't include being talked down to or being manipulated. It doesn't include being lied to or cheated on. We cannot create a gray area where we allow exceptions for people. The gray areas of life are murky and can be troublesome. "Well I make people angry" or "I don't listen, that's why they did this to me" are not valid reasons for people to repeatedly treat us badly. Enough is enough. You don't deserve this. Trust me, God has better in store for you.

" For I know the plans I have for you," declares the LORD, 'plans to prosper you and not harm you, plans to give you hope and a future' " Jeremiah 29:11.

If you habitually treat me like trash, let me do both of us a favor and take myself out of this situation!

If you are in an abusive relationship where your life is in danger, please seek help from a professional, as you plan an exit strategy.

It's time to change, our lives are at stake.

You are a prize, let your value shine.

Know when it's time to change and adjust bad habits.

❧ Share your Thoughts ❧

5

SHINE BEFORE YOU GRIND

I always remember being a multitasker. Trying to do so much at once that it felt as if I was accomplishing nothing. Life was always this hectic juggling act that often got the best of me. I would take on so many different projects and would never be able to say no. I soon learned that having an overloaded schedule can be a recipe for disaster and self-neglect. Slowly, different aspects of my life began to tear at the seams. From my health to my professional career, many things were in jeopardy. My business was making me bitter. I realized that I needed to have better balance. More so, I had to become a better manager of my life, before trying to be the CEO of the world. Hence the phase: "Shine before you grind"

The Merriam-Webster dictionary defines the word *shine* as a verb and here are three definitions:
1. to give off light
2. to have a smooth surface that reflects light
3. to be very good or successful at an activity

Let's dig in!

To give off light

As you strive to make a name for yourself and make an impact on the world, you have to work on yourself as a whole. We are all a work in progress and will never be perfect. Yet that doesn't mean that we should function in dysfunction either. As the definition states, to shine means to give off light. Ask yourself these questions:

1. Do I have a positive or negative outlook on life?
2. Is my mood usually dark and negative?
3. Would I consider myself a breath of fresh air?

Remember that your attitude determines your mood. A bad attitude can lead you in a bad mood, which in turn dims your light. Ungratefulness, holding on to anger, untreated depression, persistent bitterness, negativity and hate are all "anti-shine" behaviors and traits. That is why seeking help and having wise counsel can aid and alleviate erratic behaviors and allow us to shine. What kind of energy waves are you sending off? Is it unresolved dysfunction or are you working toward personal progress? Light is better than darkness and we must put more effort into shining as brightly as possible, putting our best selves out.

"In the same way, let your light shine before others, that they may see your good deeds and glorify your Father in heaven" Matthew 5.16.

To have a smooth surface that reflects light

God is the light and we must be able to reflect His light. Often times the rough spots in our lives hinder us from reflecting God's light. This is why we must let go of baggage and release our burdens to God on a daily basis. Baggage includes past issues or toxic people we carry around. Make a list of past hurts and shortcomings that you still have an attachment to.

_____

_____

_____

_____

_____

_____

Release those rough areas to God. Allow your heart and mind to be renewed so that you can shine!

"Create in me a clean heart, O God; and renew a right spirit within me" Psalm 51:10, KJV.

We can't shine if we have tons of baggage and hang-ups obscuring the way. Let the Son's light shine on you! Life will always have trials that will make the road rough. Surrendering the excess baggage to God will make the journey lighter and brighter.

To be very good or successful at an activity

How good are you at what you do? Do you have the spirit of excellence? In order to shine in different areas of our lives, we have to increase our level of skill and expertise. Aim to shine. What you lack in skill you must leverage with your willpower. Be great at what you do and aim to strive for your personal best. What areas do you excel in? When do you shine?

_____

_____

_____

_____

_____

_____

It's time to up the ante, to set higher standards and goals. Allow your level of skill and talent to be elevated by your determination to be the best. Time to shine brighter!

"Whatever you do, work at it with all your heart, as working for the Lord, not for human masters, since you know that you will receive an inheritance from the

Lord as a reward. It is the Lord Christ you are serving" Colossians 3:23, 24. Put your best into all you do. Put your soul into it. Shine in all your efforts and maximize your willpower. Sharpen your skills with training and coaching. Increase your drive and you will shine.

Shine before You Grind

Now that you're shining, it's time to start grinding!

The word *grind* has, in recent years, taken on a new meaning. It means to work HARD and tirelessly toward an objective.

Everyone is on the "grind" nowadays. Fighting for a dream. Pushing past obstacles. Making things happen.

Some people even believe in the "no sleep only focus" concept. My new concept is "Shine before you grind."

Shine before you grind: make yourself a priority even as you strive to get *things* done. We are so goal-oriented that we lost sight of our very soul and essence. Before you take on the work and go hard in the paint, there are some areas of your life that should be balanced. The basketball analogy, "go hard in the paint" refers to all the action that goes on in that painted rectangle right beneath the basket. One must have confidence and stamina to make the slam dunks of life. Some people believe that you should grind and then you will eventually shine, but my concept is the opposite. The desire to change the status quo is harder

when we haven't balanced out some key areas in our lives.
Make sure to give some T.L.C (tender loving care) to your mind, body, and soul as you grind. Shine from the inside out and your grind/work will be more efficient. As I stated earlier, dysfunction doesn't work well with personal development. The grind of life can burn you out if you don't have the right internal mechanisms in place. You need strength of character and grit! Building your inner core must include a detox from toxic people, environments and mindsets. Meditate, pray, set up a spa day, do your daily devotional, take yourself on a date; do things that allow you to de-stress and enhance your inner self. As you aim to climb the corporate ladder, and aim to be the best spouse or friend, you can neglect yourselves. Mark 8:36 states it plainly,
"For what will it profit a man if he gains the whole world, and loses his own soul?" (NKJV).

So dust off you old attitudes and polish your character to shine brightly. Then you can work on the other elements.

Time to do some assessment. Take some time to analyze certain areas of your life.

Instructions: Write 3 things you can do to improve each specific area. (*Start on the next page→*)

Your spirituality: Relationship with God

_____

_____

_____

_____

_____

_____

Your health: Mental and Physical

_____

_____

_____

_____

_____

Your attitude: Demeanor and Manner

_____

_____

_____

_____

_____

Your wardrobe: Head to Toe Game

_____

_____

_____

_____

_____

_____

Your skills: Education and Vocation

_____

_____

_____

_____

_____

Your purpose: Passion and Persistence

_____

_____

_____

_____

_____

Your support system: Friends and Mentors

_____

_____

_____

_____

_____

_____

Your finances: Savings and Investments

_____

_____

_____

_____

_____

_____

YOU CAN DO THIS!

❧ Share your Thoughts ❧

_____

_____

_____

_____

_____

_____

_____

_____

_____

_____

_____

_____

_____

_____

_____

_____

_____

_____

_____

_____

_____

_____

_____

_____

_____

6

CIRCLE OF INFLUENCE

I remember a time when I allowed people to continuously drain me and bring me down. I couldn't say no when I needed to, and I was constantly trying to come to the rescue of people I had no business trying to save. I soon realized I needed to work on my circle of influence. Who were the people lifting me up? I needed people in my life who would celebrate me and help me grow. Once I came to that realization, I had to assess the role I allowed people to play in my life and vice versa. Some people were not meant to stay, meaning they were just supposed to be in my life for a season, not a lifetime. Some people were just meant to teach me one life lesson, and I allowed them to take me through unnecessary drama. I gave people too much power over my thoughts and actions. I've always been the person who helps people but I rarely found people who helped me when I needed it. As I was nearing my breaking point, I realized I needed to improve and adjust the people who were in my circle. People who weighed me down or who constantly popped in and out of my life needed to be re-evaluated and escorted out of my life. I realized I deserve to be celebrated, not just tolerated.

Think and reflect on the next series of questions. It's time to strengthen your circle of influence.

Who Is in Your Circle?

Your circle can be defined as the individuals who are the closest to you. Those who have a direct impact on your life. They can include your friends, family members, and even colleagues. Trust is key in this circle. These people are basically the trustees of your life and can be held accountable for your well-being and progress. It's time to evaluate the people in your circle. Their role can dramatically enhance or decrease the quality of your life. Therefore these people need to be identified. You have to know who your resources are.

Who Is in Your Network?

Your network can include a variety of powerful contacts you maintain a relationship with. People who excel in a particular area and who can give counsel or connect you to greater resources. It's powerful when the people in your network are linked to your passion and can give you direction towards your purpose. When you need a specific task done, your network should help you make it happen. Going to networking events and volunteering will allow you to acquire a variety of contacts in different fields. Your network directly impacts your net worth. Remember it's not only who you know but who knows you!

Who Is Pouring into You?

Everyone needs a boost of encouragement from time to time. Mentors and advisors are essential when you are moving toward success. Whether it be in relationships or professional endeavors, we need to identify who our mentors are. Who are the people who can give you sound advice? We need people with discernment and expertise to be sounding boards in our lives. One or two mentors are needed. These individuals should be interested in your progress and should actively assist you in reaching greatness. Mentors and advisors are seasoned and have a wide range of experience. They take the time to ensure you are progressing in your endeavors because they more than likely have already walked down the path you are now traveling.

Who Influences You to Make Positive Decisions?

Do not be misled, "Bad company corrupts good character" 1 Corinthians 15:33. Friends and acquaintances should lead you toward higher heights, not the pits. Spiritual leaders are also key in steering us back to God. We must surround ourselves with people who can help us make positive decisions. People who will tell us the truth in a loving way. Individuals who will encourage and chastise us in love. Some people in our lives claim to love us, but they constantly lead us to poor decisions. We need to be influenced by people who aim high, not low.

Who Is Helping Open Doors for You?

God opens doors for us. He leads us to the right opportunities when we surrender to His will. God uses people to create opportunities for His children. What individuals in your life are in high places of influence and can prepare the way for you? We all know it's not always what you know but who knows you and can make that one phone call. Align yourself with trusted people of power and influence. Pray for divine guidance and discernment to meet the right people who can help usher change in your life. How many CEOs or executives do you know? It's time to do some networking and get connected. You'll be surprised by how many influential people are in your contact list. Or you may know somebody who knows somebody who knows somebody . . .

Time for Action

Prayer and faith initiate things in our lives. We listen for God's direction and then walk with divine authority. God will lead you to cut the things and people who drain you and suck you dry. Trust the process and be brave. Seek people who are in the area of your purpose and can help elevate you. You have to get in where you fit in. Cut off the leeches and vampires in your life, it is easier said than done, but it's definitely doable.

Make a general list of your power-contacts. Reconnect with them today!

❧ Share your Thoughts ❧

_____

_____

_____

_____

_____

_____

_____

_____

_____

_____

_____

_____

_____

_____

_____

_____

_____

_____

_____

_____

_____

_____

_____

7

STAY MOTIVATED

For as long as I could remember, I've always struggled with my weight and making healthy food choices. My favorite pastime would always be to stock up on all my favorite junk foods and just pig out. This was my comfort zone. My go-to. With the woe of failure looming and a lack of direction, I delved deeper into my unhealthy way of living. My dysfunctional relationship with food was creating all sorts of problems. Depression and anxiety often weighted me down and I often felt like food was my only comfort. Whenever I felt overwhelmed or disappointed, food was my hero. When I felt happy or excited, food was my buddy to celebrate with. It wasn't until my body started attacking itself that I realized I needed a real change. I would have all these aches and pains throughout the whole day. Debilitating muscle pain and headaches. I felt desolate and helpless. It wasn't until I had a consultation with a good friend of mine who was a naturalist that I realized the foods I was eating were poisoning my body. I had to make a decision. I had to transition to a healthier lifestyle. Mentally and physically, it all had to change. As I continue this journey to become healthier, one thing does remain consistent . . . I have to stay motivated. I have to remind myself that I am worth more than any cookie or bag of chips. I have to stay determined. The quality of my life depends on it. So here are some tips I am using.

Mix it Up

Target and analyze different aspects of your goal. If you have been trying the same thing for an extended period of time and have gotten no positive results, then it's time to mix it up. It is good to have a routine because it keeps you consistent. Yet, you can get bored easily. Boredom can lead to wondering off the positive track. So finding creative ways to add spice to your routine can be a life changer. For better health, I have to exercise daily. Somedays I go to gym, other days I work up a good sweat creating dance routines. Either way, I have to mix things up every now and then. Whether it's your social life or your meal planning, research some things that can add some fire and motivation to the mix. This will keep you on your toes and at the top of your game. No room for mediocrity or for the mundane things of life. It's time to mix it up!

Go Hard

Increase your time of execution and be more intentional. Kiss procrastination goodbye and amp up your level of effort. Increase your level of intensity.

Monitor and keep track of your success daily. Sometimes we get so lazy that we completely stop progressing. Give it all you have, because you often only get one shot in life. Basketball players are familiar with the painted rectangular area right underneath the basket. Commentators usually refer to players "going hard in the paint". I love this concept! This painted rectangle is where a lot of action happens to guarantee that the team scores a shot. In order to make those slam dunks in life, you must go hard in the paint. Push past the obstacles with confidence and give your maximum effort.

Branch Out

When promoting a business, find new marketing platforms. When selling a new product line, find new venues to sale it. Don't limit yourself. You are a creative being with interesting ideas and concepts. Oftentimes we feel stuck, but we have to push and get out of our comfort zone. When setting goals, it is always good to stay focused. Finding ways to reach the next level should always be your goal. Aim for higher heights and branch out.

Get Some ZZZ's

If you are not well-rested you can't function at your optimal level. Sleep is essential because it's the time when the cells in your body rejuvenate. As you stay motivated and push, factor in time for some good rest. Then you will be refreshed and energized for the tasks that are ahead. I would have insomnia when planning a big event. Nerves would get the best of me and I couldn't wind down. So I had to find a calming routine. Developing a night time routine can help you fall asleep faster. Turn off your electronic devices, get some calming tea. Find music that soothes you mind. Pray or read scriptures to re-center your mind. Some can function with little to no sleep, but understand that your body needs to refuel. Sleep is essential for cells in your body to function optimally. Rest your mind, body and soul!

Develop an Attitude of Gratitude

"Give thanks in all circumstances; for this is God's will for you in Christ Jesus" 1 Thessalonians 5:18.

Giving thanks and being grateful shouldn't only be reserved for birthdays and holidays. We should daily express our thanks and practice having an attitude of gratitude. This will allow us to stay motivated as we look forward to greater things to come. It's hard to stay motivated if you consistently feel bitter and resentful. This is one of the reasons why developing an attitude of gratitude is essential for success. When you consider all the things and people in your life you should be grateful. This will motivate you to push forward.

Life is like a camera . . .

Focus *on what's important*

Capture *the good times*

Develop *from the negatives*

And if things don't work out

Take another shot

—Anonymous

❧ Share your Thoughts ❧

_____

_____

_____

_____

_____

_____

_____

_____

_____

_____

_____

_____

_____

_____

_____

_____

_____

_____

_____

_____

_____

_____

_____

_____

_____

8

LIVE YOUR WORTH

Grade school was brutal. I was always the last one picked as teams were formed for dodge ball. When the love grams were sent for Valentine's Day I never received one from a secret admirer. Even compliments were very hard to come by. But when I fell in love with God, I found my identity in Him. A child of the King. A princess. Royalty. With unique gifts and talents that made me unique in His kingdom. I knew I was important. The hard part was living my worth when the going got tough, when people disrespected and disregarded me, when I was rejected and ignored, when my talents were overlooked. I had to develop the mindset that no matter what situation I found myself in, I was going to exercise my worth. To exercise my God given qualities at every turn. At every moment, and with every person. I had to learn and understand that my worth was not up for debate. I had to live like I deserved God's best every day. Living my worth allowed my destiny to be activated. "For the Spirit God gave us does not make us timid, but gives us power, love and self-discipline" 2 Timothy 1:7.

Walk in the Knowledge of Who You Are

Who are you? You are a child of the King of kings, and that makes you royalty. You are heir to the throne.

1 Peter 2:9 says, "But you are a chosen generation, a royal priesthood, a holy nation, His own special people; that you may proclaim the praises of Him who called you out of darkness into his marvelous light" (NKJV).

This is awesome news! Understanding who you are in the sight of God is essential to walking in your value. When you realize that the God of the universe holds you in such high esteem, you can be empowered by His declaration.

"I praise you because I am fearfully and wonderfully made; your works are wonderful. I know that fully well" Psalm 139:14.

You are wonderfully made in the image of God and that solidifies your worth. You are a valuable treasure. You are not a cheap knock-off or a shabby clearance item. Recognize your worth and don't allow people to put a sales price tag on a precious gem. You are priceless. Worth far more than any ruby. In order to live your worth you have to first know your value and know who you are. Next you have to believe that you are valuable. Your value is divinely established and validated. Lastly, you have to put your belief in action.

You have to activate your value system and live your worth. Once your value is set, let nothing depreciate it. Living your worth is a day to day operation. It starts with a daily attitude check that trickles down to how you treat yourself and others. Acknowledge, believe and activate your worth.

Self-Esteem and Self-Confidence

When you know who you are, how you feel about yourself can't be shaken by naysayers. Walk in the knowledge of who you are.

Have confidence and boldness through faith in Christ. (Ephesians 3:12)

You are complete in Christ (Colossians 3:1)

You are a child of God (John 1:12)

You are accepted by Christ (Romans 8:17)

You are triumphant (2 Corinthians 2:14)

You are not your past (Galatians 3:28)

You are free (Galatians 5:1)

You are chosen (1 Thessalonians 1:4)

You are loved (John 3:16)

You are blessed (Philippians 4:19)

You are victorious (Revelation 12:11)

You are forgiven (Ephesians 1:7)

Every moment requires confidence and you don't need to fake it. Instead faith it. Believe in what God says about you. You are the head and not the tail, above and not beneath, a lender not a borrower (Deuteronomy 28:12,13). Believe in your God-given qualities and attributes. Be self-confident in all environments and at all times. Walk in your purpose. Live out your mission. Tramp over the snakes and scorpions of your life, you have the authority (Luke 10:19). No more shying away from your purpose because you doubt your worth. Live out Loud!

Philippians 4:13 "I can do all things through Christ who strengthens me."

Humility

There is a huge difference between confidence and cockiness; humility is the missing piece between the two. You can be confident while staying grounded by humility. Be humble. C.S. Lewis was quoted in saying, "True humility is not thinking less of yourself, it's thinking of yourself less." Live your worth by recognizing the impact it has on others. No one needs to be belittled in order for your value to be elevated. You never need to tear anyone down to build yourself up. Luke 14:11 says, "For whoever exalts himself will be humbled, and he who humbles himself will be exalted" (NKJV). Live your worth in humility and you will always prosper.

Diamonds Shine No Matter What

People will constantly test you and throw proverbial dirt on your value. This is an effort to diminish your worth and make you live in doubt of your greatness. Diamonds shine no matter what the environment. You are far more valuable than any jewel or stone. So keep your head held high and walk through life with this knowledge. Regardless of the obstacles in your life, **SHINE**. No matter how dark certain circumstances may get, **SHINE**. Whether or not people support you, **SHINE**. Regardless of your past, **SHINE**. Through the pain and the rain, **SHINE!**

Live It

When people doubt you, live your worth. When people disregard your presence, live your worth. When others try to intimidate you, live your worth. Don't settle for a dead-end job. Live your worth. Don't envy the success and beauty of others. Live your worth. When you want to quit, live your worth. When people turn their backs on you, live your worth. When you feel there are no real opportunities, live your worth. When you have no friends, live your worth. When you are having a bad day, live your worth. When you don't feel valued, live your worth. No matter the environment. Live your worth. No matter the people. Let the light that God has placed within you shine before all man, so that you Heavenly Father will be gloried (see 1 Peter 4:11).

Don't just say you are worth it. Act like you know you are! Never downplay who God has called you to be.

Your worth can not be dependent on someone else's view of you. Push past obstacles of disrespect and rejection. Don't let anyone define you. Another person might not always see what God sees in you, and that's ok.

LIVE YOUR WORTH!

I'm choosing to live my worth

And pushing past the hurt

I have decided that I'm not going back

To living in misery and in lack

My life is full of abundance and joy

I have all I need, I fret no more

My life is in full bloom, I see that light

It shines bright even in the dark of night

Walking in the knowledge of who I was created to be

I am more than a conqueror, You wait and see

-Daniela

❧ Share your Thoughts ❧

_____

_____

_____

_____

_____

_____

_____

_____

_____

_____

_____

_____

_____

_____

_____

_____

_____

_____

_____

_____

_____

_____

_____

9

A.P.E. MODE

ASSESS. PLAN. EXECUTE

Everyone remembers the movie King Kong. The story of the giant gorilla who whisks the beautiful damsel into the forest and is eventually hunted and killed. This was a tragic story of the animal kingdom and mankind colliding. Though we all wish things had ended differently for Kong, one thing is clear, he didn't go down without a fight. As I reflected on this, an interesting acronym came to my mind. A.P.E. Assess. Plan. Execute. Life's best successes occur when we walk in purpose and activate A.P.E. Mode.

Assess

It's time to make a thorough assessment of the direction your life is heading towards. When was the last time you decided to pause and evaluate your practices? Maybe you can go to the park with a journal and assess different aspects of your life. And be totally honest with yourself. Is it finally time for change? Take a deeper look at the last 6 month or the past 5 years. And be totally honest with yourself. Is it finally time for a transformation? Is it time to shift gears? Yes, it's time. Things in life can be frustrating and difficult to manage. Assessing your life is a good way to regain control. There may be multiple areas that you need to focus on. Simply make a list of things and then prioritize them. Zeroing in on certain key areas can make a huge impact in your life. When our lives get out of sync the first step is to make an assessment of things. You may have to assess your passions and hobbies to discover your purpose. Maybe you need to reassess your daily routines and habits because they are ineffective. Sometimes it's your time management that may need to be adjusted. It may even be time to assess you professional career and to repurpose your current position. Find a quiet space and start to assess! With prayer, meditation and introspection, great things will be revealed.

Plan

Now it's time for some strategy. Formulating an effect plan will take your life to the next level. Proverbs 16:3 is clear, "Commit to the Lord whatever you do, and he will establish your plans." As you begin to decipher how to move closer to success, you must stay vigilant and pray. Planning and strategizing can get quite daunting. Outline key objectives and map out each step. Outlining a clear course of action takes wisdom and research. As you plan and brainstorm, seek God's voice for divine strategy. Keep track of your planning through detailed notes and calendar entries. Planning is where you see in detail what steps are needed to be taken to accomplish a particular task. Though you can't foresee every problem, planning gives you an advantage nonetheless. As you assess the different task that need to be accomplished in your life, you will soon realize that you have to plan specifically for each goal. Live your worth by leaving nothing to chance. Step by step, task by task, formulate a plan of action. Vibrant, play-by-play steps will bring you one step closer to success. We all need a road map! A wise man once said if you fail to plan, you plan to fail.

Execute

Now it's time to roll up those sleeves and get those hands dirty. Nike's slogan sums it up quite nicely, "Just Do It".

Now that you've given yourself the opportunity to find your unique contribution to the world, it's time to let your purpose make progress. It's time to execute your plan and put strategizes in motion. Once you start executing your assessed plan, you will start seeing things shift in your life. Your dreams will be actualized. A fulfilled life will emerge. You have the road map, so now it's time to execute your plan of action. Begin to execute one step at a time. Developing a checklist for each particular task can be extremely valuable. Track your progress and quantify your results. Manage your success by keeping track of your completed tasks. Pace yourself. Life is a marathon not a sprint.

It's about remembering that you are worth the change that will be produced by your efforts. Things are easier said than done, but definitely doable. Persistency and consistency will pay off. Cross those things off your To-Do List or Not-Do List. (Not-Do-List includes things in your life that you want to stop doing and need a friendly reminded). Prioritize and you will be surprised at how evident your progress will be. It's time to go into A.P.E Mode. Your future awaits. Remember that goals without plans are wishes. And plans without execution are just fluff. A motto I would like for you to recite is "Easier said than done but doable". This motto is tied to Philippians 4:13, "I can do all things through Christ who gives me strength." Your goals and objectives may seem difficult to obtain, fear not, you've got this. Persistency and consistency will pay off, so don't lose hope. Keep climbing. Keep pushing. You've come too far to quit now.

What are the top three things in your life you need to go A.P.E on? List them and Let's get it done!

❧ Share your Thoughts ❧

_____

_____

_____

_____

_____

_____

_____

_____

_____

_____

_____

_____

_____

_____

_____

_____

_____

_____

_____

_____

_____

_____

_____

10

DON'T BE THIRSTY

In my early-twenties, I became obsessed with the desire to be in a relationship. My every waking thought and brain activity was geared toward my hopes of finding my soul mate. None of the guys I met had potential and this was making me extremely impatient. I was literary young and restless. I felt totally engulfed by this. Then came the obsession of being accepted by people. I wanted everyone to be my friend. I gave people access to my life who had no business being in my space. And with the combination of both of these obsessions, disaster ensued. It is fair to say that my soul was yearning for companionship in all the wrong places. I was desperate. I was thirsty. After seeking some wise counsel. I was reminded to seek God first. I started praying for God to quench my thirst. I started asking God to fill, hydrate and saturate me with His love and acceptance. My thirst for God was re-ignited. I was satisfied.

The word thirsty has taken on a whole new meaning. It no longer is a word that only describes that dryness in your throat on a hot summer day. Now when people refer to each other as "thirsty," it signifies that you are desperately yearning for something or someone that is not within your grasp. When someone now uses the word thirsty, it may refer to the observation that all your actions overly exude desperation and longing. When your body is physically dehydrated, you may experience symptoms of dizziness, dry mouth or even a headache. This may be an indication that you need water. Your body slowly begins to lose proper function. Likewise, when you are feeling desperate or "thirsty" your mind and body begin to function in an erratic state. You can't think clearly and often act on impulse.

When the pressures of life start to escalate, it may be difficult to remain levelheaded. Exceling in one area of your life and failing miserably in another can be challenging. This imbalance may cause us to be impatient. This impatience may lead us to become anxious. Anxiety may sometimes lead to desperation. Many like to use the phrase, "desperate times call for desperate measures." Our desires can soon overtake our logic, leading us to take desperate measures. All of this is a vicious cycle. There is still hope. Trusting

God's ultimate plan relieves our anxiety and eliminates our hopelessness. John 4:14 says, "But whoever drinks of the water that I will give him will never be thirsty again" (ESV). When I start feeling frantic and thirsty, I recite one of my favorite verses, Proverb 3:5-6, "Trust in the Lord with all your heart and lean not to thy own understanding, in all your ways acknowledge Him and he will make your paths" (KJV). I remind myself that my Heavenly Father has my back and knows best what I need. This helps quench my thirst and reignite my worth. It's a minute by minute process for me on some days. This is when I have to constantly go to my Heavenly water source. And God reminds me to trust Him, for He is still looking out for me. I am worthy of more and can never settle for less. Crumbs will not due, I must accept His best. Though life may seem bitter, God wants me to shift my perspective and start seeing things in a positive light.

Making lemonade from the lemons of life is a must in keeping your thirst quenched. At times, I look at the lemons and I just want Kool-Aid. I found a remedy for this problem. Prayer, praise, and reading the word of God are the elements that make life sweeter. So when life gets bitter, use your spiritual sweeteners to quench your soul. Through the Living Water you get a spiritual detox. When you stay hydrated in Christ, desperation, dehydration, and despair will be transformed to determination, ambition, and drive.

Remember that God delights in His creation. He wants us to be content. "Delight yourself in the Lord, and he will give you the desires of your heart" Psalm 34:11, ESV.

There is nothing to be ashamed about when you feel thirsty. God gave us these longings and desires. The catch is, He wants to be the one to quench them for us.

"You, God, are my God, earnestly I seek you; I thirst for you; my whole being longs for you, in a dry and parched land where there is no water" Psalm 63:1, NIV.

Take a moment and express your gratitude. Take a moment and simply say THANK YOU. Appreciate where you are in life and trust the process. God will keep His promises to you. Just wait and see. Often, we worry about what isn't coming our way. We obsess over what hasn't happened yet, but we must remember that when we worry, we negate our trust in God. He doesn't want us to thirst for worldly things, but to thirst for His presence. Three things can help us stay quenched. Prayer, praise, and a passionate relationship with God. Reading His word will intensify this relationship. When we learn God's character and crave a relationship with Him, things shift in our lives. We are no longer dependent on any other source for affirmation, security or acceptance. God will quench our thirst. As Psalm 147:3 declares, "He heals the brokenhearted and binds up their wounds." Remind yourself that there is a greater calling on your life. This calling must be fulfilled through your unique purpose. So as you patiently wait, let God co-sign for you. Do not rely on others for affirmation, acceptance, or assurance. Instead trust God to lead you to the right opportunities.

Here are a few spiritual sweeteners that will relief your thirst:

Sweetener #1 PRAYER

Prayer is direct communication with God. If we are not communicating with God, we cannot discern the path He wants us to take. Prayer open doors and faith allows us to walk through them. Funny how we can talk on the phone for hours but can't talk to God for five whole minutes! Not only do we need to speak to God in prayer, we need to actively listen through meditation and quiet time to receive His answers.

Sweetener #2 PRAISE

Praise pleases God and is a major line of defense against the attacks of the Enemy. When you have an attitude of praise and gratitude to the Lord it changes the outlook of any situation. Worshipping God through our lifestyle is also essential. Keep praise in your heart and a song on your lips.

Sweetener #3 PERUSE

The Bible is the manual for our relationship with God. His character is revealed more and more as we read the Bible. We experience His love as we read His word. Great revelation and relief can be found in the word of God. Find his promises, browse through His extensive resume. Read His Word for assurance and accept the love He has for you. His record is good!

Only God can quench our desires and thirsty souls. Daily we should thirst for His presence. Even when things feel hopeless and the well of life looks dry, let us look to our ULTIMATE source of living water! Be thirsty no more.

❧ Share your Thoughts ❧

_____

_____

_____

_____

_____

_____

_____

_____

_____

_____

_____

_____

_____

_____

_____

_____

_____

_____

_____

_____

_____

_____

_____

_____

_____

_____

_____

11

DRAMA AND TRAUMA

As a child and well into my adult years, I experienced a great deal of verbal and emotional abuse. Words that tore my self-worth to pieces. Words that still to this day resonate in my ear. Repeatedly hearing that I was not good enough, skinny enough, or smart enough slowly eroded my self-worth. As my self-worth eroded, I began to experience an identity crisis. I didn't know who I was. Whatever people said about me was what I believed. Good or bad, I absorbed it into my identity. The trauma of the verbal abuse led to drama in my interpersonal life. I soon caught myself destroying others through the same weapons of belittlement and depreciation that I had experienced growing up. It was a vicious cycle. The healing and growth that took place was truly miraculous. I can truly say that God has renewed my mind and heart, and restored my identity. Though I am often tested, I rely solely on Christ for my identity. Now I repeat the affirming words that my Heavenly Father says about me. The wounds have healed.

We all have been through one form of abuse or another; physical abuse, sexual abuse, bullying, dating violence, family violence, threats, assault, molestation or rape. This abuse leaves deep-seated trauma. Our core is shaken and pain grips our mind and body. The wounds and pain that stems from abuse can last a lifetime, but this doesn't have to be the case. Time and therapy can help the healing process. It is quite necessary to speak to licensed professionals in order to heal from the wounds of abuse. The wounds will eventually heal with time, therapy and prayer. Most wounds leave scars, but these scars are a testament to your resilience and strength. Even Jesus has scars on His hands, proof that He conquered hell, death, and sin! You are a conqueror. A winner. Triumphant. Your pain will lead to growth. These growing pains are not ideal put it's part of the process. Your scars don't dictate who you are destined to be.

Oprah Winfrey is a world-renowned talk show host. Her net worth is currently estimated at $3 Billion. She created her own television network, magazine, and empowers billions of people around the world. But Oprah's life has not been without trauma and pain. At the age of nine she was raped by her teenage cousin, and in the years to follow, she was sexually abused by various members of her family. Oprah's successes superseded the pain and abuse of her past. One of Oprah's famous quote is *"Turn your wounds into wisdom.*" The wisdom that came from her pains ushered her into her purpose. Though the road was full of obstacles and heartbreak, she overcame. You too can overcome.

You too have a story of pain. Wherever you are in the world, no matter your educational level or your faith, you have experienced trauma. Whether emotional or physical, you may be living with deep wounds. It's time to claim your healing and let go of the pain. It's time to open the chapter of healing in your life. Claim your breakthrough now. No longer do you have to be tormented by your past. It's time to release the darkness that binds you. Your self-worth has been destroyed and mutilated. Your mind may be troubled and your heart broken. Remember that healing is available. You may not know where to begin the healing process. Repeat this out loud,

"I LET IT GO"
"THIS HURT DOESN'T DEFINE ME"
"I AM HEALED"
"I HAVE PEACE"
Take a deep breathe in, hold it for a few seconds and slowly release.

Now take some time to pray and journal your thoughts.

Another great step would be to find a licensed professional who can offer you some therapy sessions.

73

If you don't have the finances for such a move, speak to a trusted spiritual leader with a background in counseling. If you have had thoughts of suicide call the national hotline at 1-800-273-8255.

Don't give up on your healing and breakthrough. Your future depends on it. You no longer have to endure the abuse and neglect of people in your life. In order to live your purpose you must be freed from the past hurts that plague you. Healing is available. Don't hurt in silence anymore. You are more than worth it. Speak out and be healed.

● THREATS OF PHYSICAL HARM ● CONSTANT CRITICISM
● SPITEFUL COMMENTS ● PUBLIC SHAMING ● BELITTLING ● RIDICULE
● MAKING FUN OF APPEARANCE OR ABILITY ● LABELING
● REPEATEDLY POINTING OUT MISTAKES ● INTENTIONAL EMBARRASSING
● PUT-DOWNS DISGUISED AS JOKES ● TEASING ● NAME-CALLING
● BLAME-SHIFTING ● FAULT-FINDING ● GOSSIPING
● LASHING OUT ● YELLING ● HUMILIATING ● INSULTING

EMOTIONAL ABUSE

underlies physical abuse, sexual abuse, bullying, dating violence, family violence, and all forms of human cruelty & unkindness.

● SCAPE-GOATING ● HOSTILE LOOKS ● SARCASM ● INDIFFERENCE
● GIVING THE "SILENT TREATMENT" ● SNIDE REMARKS
● WITHHOLDING AFFECTION & EMOTIONAL SUPPORT ● PICKING FIGHTS
● LYING ● REFUSING TO TALK & LISTEN ● ANGRY ATTACKS
● DISMISSING ONE'S IDEAS & OPINIONS ● UNFLATTERING NICKNAMES
● IGNORING ● REJECTION ● BETRAYAL ● EMOTIONAL ABANDONMENT
● ISOLATING FROM SUPPORTIVE FRIENDS & FAMILY
● MAKING ONE FEEL INFERIOR, NOT 'GOOD ENOUGH', WORTHLESS

focusas.org

❧ Share your Thoughts ❧

_____

_____

_____

_____

_____

_____

_____

_____

_____

_____

_____

_____

_____

_____

_____

_____

_____

_____

_____

_____

_____

_____

_____

_____

_____

12

YOU ARE NOT A FRACTION, YOU ARE WHOLE

I often think of the things or features that would make me feel more complete, like a brand new car with a navigation system, leather seats and a sunroof; we all like added features. In my own life, I want features too. I refer to these features as the "dream package". The dream package consists of my dream job, owning my own home, a devoted soul mate, two kids, cool friends and great health. I daydream that my life would probably be more enjoyable if I had my dream package. I would feel more complete, comfortable and fulfilled. My self-worth would miraculously be catapulted to extreme heights. I would have the things that the majority of the population desires. I would be content. WAIT! Hear me out. I'm not naïve enough to believe that these features could guarantee my happiness. The dream package comes with its own set of problems and headaches, but still, a girl can dream. NEWS FLASH! I am complete without any added features. My worth isn't tied to the extra features of life such as a job, a brand new car or a beau. In fact, the ability to live my worth through all the qualities and abilities I was born with, is more than enough. Life is like a box of chocolates, you have to sink your teeth in to discover what's really inside. It may take a few bitter attempts, but you will eventually find that sweet spot within! Once you recognize your worth and live it out, you will finish strong and realize that the strength that brought you through was already within you. Through the pains and delays of life, remember that it's never too late to be the person you were called to be. Your destiny is greater than your history.

Image

With all that the media portrays, it's easy to lose your identity. The celebrities and internet sensations have everyone in search of the perfect body. How can one feel complete with cellulite, a gut, and double chin? Society wants you to be as perfect as it pretends to be. The pressure heightens as we post pictures or videos on our social media pages, and wait for the world to like, share and repost. No longer must we live in fear of what others expect of us. The only image that we should aim to reflect is that of our Maker. Look in the mirror, you are flawsome and perfectly you. OWN your IMAGE!

flawsome:
[*flô-sэm*] adjective

an individual who embraces their "flaws" and knows
they are awesome regardless.

Motivation

Stay motivated because getting to the finish line of your goals is worth it. Though the road may get rough, stay empowered. You can stay motivated by finding the things that ignite you. Don't get frustrated by delays and denials. Keep producing greatness. There are no limits to what you can achieve when you stay motivated.

Explore Unfamiliar Territory

Discover new parts of yourself by venturing into the unknown. Keep an open mind and broaden your outlook. Bulk up your confidence and hit the ground running. Explore new places and expand your horizons. Leave your comfort zone behind. That's the only way to enhance your life. Elevate your life by discovering new places that will enhance your purpose. The more you venture out, the more you will gain from your life.

Fuel Yourself

Don't allow your passions to fizzle. Work on your dreams as diligently as you do your day job. Stay the course it will soon pay off. Trust the process because it is building your character. Fuel your purpose and fulfill your God-given mission. This will increase your sense of worth. Fuel your value by exploring your passions. Be bold and operate in your worth. Don't downplay yourself.

Get Clarity

It's time to clear the pathway of your life to get a clear vision of what's next in your life. Take some quiet time to reflect, meditate and pray. You will receive the vision that God has for your life. Get away from the noise and everything that brings drama to your life. Remove the excess to claim your success.

Positivity Rocks

It's time to shift gears and get in a positive mindset. There are plenty of things to be negative about. Negativity can easily bring you down into a dark pit. To feel complete, you have to be content with the contents of your life and express an attitude of gratitude. Renew your mind and stay positive. Look at life through positive lenses and things will eventually look up.

Determination

Staying determined can take a lot of concentration. Especially when the obstacles of life get higher and steeper. Stay the course! The mountains may seem hard to climb, but you can conquer them one step at a time. Face your fears even when you smell failure brewing. Failure is sometimes inevitable. So don't focus on it. Instead, when you fall, dust yourself off, learn the lessons from the situation and keep moving. Turn your fears into fuel and keep on trucking.

Develop Your Beliefs

What is the source of your faith? What do you plug into daily to get that boost? It's time to start making time to strengthen your faith. Who are you plugging into that drain your beliefs and value systems? Identity those people and unplug. Find your spiritual source and plug in. Plug in through prayer. Plug in by meditating on the Word. Know what you believe in and be grounded through faith. Experience God daily.

Be Ready for the Ride

Once you align yourself with faith, favor and fervor, things in your life will begin to take off. Always remember that life is a journey, things come in their appropriate seasons. You can't rush the change, but you can be ready when the opportunity comes. Be ready and seize every unique opportunity that comes your way. And while you're at it go ahead and create some opportunities for yourself. Demand respect and reflect on the person you have been called to be. STAY READY. The faith and fire within you will take you anywhere you want to go.

Pave a New Path

Out with the old and in with the new! It's time to find new inspiration to revive your energy. Accept who you are and make your own path to success. Surprise yourself by showing off your best qualities and attributes. You will delight and bless the masses with your newfound innovation. Life doesn't have a script, trust the process.

Willpower

Dig deep within yourself. Strap up your boots and start walking, you have everything you need within yourself. God placed it all in you. Pray for added willpower to make it through tough times. These trials can make life seem worthless and pointless. This is why you need to take a deep breath and will yourself to go for it. Willpower is the engine that propels you forward in life. You got this!

Don't give up! BE consistent. BE persistent.
YOU WILL IGNITE YOUR WORTH.
YOU ARE COMPLETE! YOU ARE WHOLE!
YOU ARE WORTH IT! SO LIVE IT! ❧

Share your Thoughts ❧

_____

_____

_____

_____

_____

_____

_____

_____

_____

_____

_____

_____

_____

_____

_____

_____

_____

_____

_____

_____

_____

_____

_____

_____

SELF- ESTEEM GUIDE

Shine Before You Grind

<u>SELF- ESTEEM GUIDE</u>

INTRO

Your self- esteem has many layers. Each layer protects

who you are at your core. Get to know yourself and the

things that make you, you! Add value to yourself and

allow no one to tear you down. Build yourself up.

Enhance your overall value.

Appreciate yourself. You are worth it.

Part 1

The Masterpiece

Affirmation

Words matter. Feed positivity to your soul. You are a masterpiece in the making, so remind yourself of that daily. No one is perfect, so just work on progressing to the next level. Don't allow others to talk down to you. And most importantly, don't talk down to yourself. What you secretly believe about yourself will show up in every aspect of your life. Know what God says about you. Repeat a positive mantra or self-written poem to yourself daily. Remind yourself who you are. The amount of likes you get on social media don't affirm you. Encourage yourself. Speak life and positivity.

I am valuable
I am the master of my own thoughts
I am courageous
I choose to live my life 100%
I live with gratitude
I am always protected
I am strong
I am perfect in my imperfections
I am opening my heart to love
I am accepting to go with the flow of life
I am receptive to all the changes in my life
I am inspired
I am ME (Masterpiece Extraordinaire)

WRITE YOUR OWN AFFIRMATIONS

_____

_____

_____

_____

_____

_____

_____

_____

_____

_____

_____

Attitude

Life presents various situations that can affect our mood, and since feelings aren't meant to control us, we must learn to experience and release them. Feelings remind us that we are human. Try not to dwell on negative emotions. Doing an attitude check, allows you to put your feelings in perspective and to have a positive demeanor. Be responsive not reactive. Slight adjustments in perceptions can help you cope with all situations. Remember that your vibe and attitude attract others to you. Don't allow a sour attitude to taint how you see yourself or your future. Let your attitude be refreshing and inviting.

Posture and Poise

Take some time to observe your posture. Rate your poise. Your stance adds to your positive self-image. When you sit up straight and stand with your shoulders back, you add a flare of confidence to your persona. Work on how you sit and stand. Try doing this in front of a mirror. When you slouch, you can be misconstrued as a lazy person or lacking confidence. It takes away from your persona and personality. Crossing your arms when in conversation can imply you are disinterested or upset. You may just be cold, but others may interpret this as insecurity or a "Don't approach me attitude." So uncross those arms! Keep your chin up and walk with confidence. Don't let your crown slip!

Eye Contact = Confidence

The eyes are the key to the soul. Believe it or not, your eyes speak volumes. They can easily express what is going on in your head. So it is important to keep eye contact with people, especially in conversation. You can express interest, intrigue and excitement with your eyes alone! Practice different emotions in the mirror. This will help you in your interactions with others. Express exactly what you want to convey. Be genuinely you.

Smile

It takes more facial muscles to frown than to smile. Your smile is your best asset, so use it to your advantage. When you smile, it puts people at ease and gives you a welcoming demeanor. So take care of those pearly whites. A dazzling smile can be a great people magnet. The world has enough problems, so why not smile. Smiling instantly makes you feel better. Remember to smile with your soul.

Check your crew

Surrounding yourself with the right people is extremely important. Finding friends who will allow you to be yourself can really boost your self-esteem. Keep your friend circle intimate and transparent. Everyone can't be privy to all the details of your life.

So choose your friends wisely. Remember that everyone is not meant to be in your life forever. Choose the right crew, find people who will celebrate you; those who aim to understand your personality and help you grow. No leeches and no bullies allowed.

Skin Care

The skin is the largest organ of the human body. It helps balance body temperature and protects internal organs. So obviously it needs extra TLC (tender loving care). A dermatologist can help you have healthier skin and can help you find the right products that best fit your skin type. Invest in quality products. If you choose to wear makeup, try not to mask but to enhance your natural features. Nothing is better than your natural self. Great skin can boost self-esteem. So find some online tutorials for day and night routine that will help your skin to glow.

Health and Fitness

Your body is a temple. Be more careful of the food and beverages you consume. Water and exercise are essential to maintaining a healthy body. When your body feels and looks good, your self-esteem gets a boost. It's time to put the excuses aside. See your physician for your annual physical to get a baseline of your health status. A nutritionist can also assist in developing a healthy meal plan to optimize your body function.

Fashion and Style

Find your personal style and enhance it! With clothing and accessories that are age and size appropriate, the sky is the limit to how great you can look. You can be modest and trendy. You can be cool and chic, while still staying true to your values. Find the right clothes to present the best reflection of your true self. Your garments can't replace your character, but should in fact reflect it. Represent yourself in the best way, in all situations.

Part 2

Self-Competition

You Are Your Own Competition

It's time to focus on yourself. Repeat after me: "I am my own competition." That's Right!

Be more concerned about your life's mission then that of others. Aim to be your best self. Don't worry so much about what others are doing. Do what you need to do to get to your best self.

Work on beating your personal best. Aim to be better than you were last year. Go bigger than you've ever gone before. Put those blinders on and go for the gold.

Conquering the Enemy and Inner Me

Oftentimes we are fighting against our own self-doubt. Self-sabotage can stop you from achieving great heights. Quit believing the lies others have lead you to believe about yourself. The devil is our enemy and is constantly trying to block us from our destiny. You are a conqueror. You are a winner. Be aware of the evil games the enemy plays. Stay prayed up and keep affirming yourself.

Stop Comparing Yourself to Others

It's extremely easy to compare your achievements to the accomplishments of others. Focusing on our neighbor's grass will not make ours greener. Instead, assess your purpose and aim to fulfill it. Stop downplaying your abilities because you are blinded by the gleam of others. When you compare yourself to others you can be easily led into despair. Focus on project YOU, then there will be no competition.

Honor Your Uniqueness

You are as unique as your fingerprints. Even identical twins don't have the same fingerprints! This means that we all can leave our unique mark on the world. Your path, purpose, and passions have specifically been assigned to you for a reason. Own it. Work it. Change the world.

Mentoring a Masterpiece

As athletes prepare for competitions, they usually train with a trainer. A coach or a guru in the field that helps prepare them for greatness. Someone who is willing to train you and pour their expertise into you is needed. This person can help polish and sharpen you for the next level of success. Mature and trustworthy, the right mentor can help you evolve.

Be a Better Version of Yourself

All software need to be updated. Think of your phone or even your computer; without the proper updates they won't function efficiently. Apps get upgraded with new features all the time. In order to get to a better version of yourself, you must upgrade to the next version. Upgrade the software of your life. This is the only way you will be able to enhance the resolution of your life.

No mediocrity. No procrastination. No hesitation. Get better. If the iPhone offer new features every year how much more should you be able to upgrade yourself?

Improve the technology of you.

Stay in Your Lane

Your purpose and skill set is unique to you. If you have been gifted with certain talents, harness them. Sharpen them. Don't try to do what everyone else is doing because it looks cool. Do what you've been designed to do. Don't try something because you secretly envy the success of others. Keep your motives and intentions pure. Focus on what you were called to do. Excel in your arena of expertise.

Embrace the Process

Rome wasn't built in a day. Greatness takes time, so

work on yourself daily. Motivate your mind and body to keep pushing even when things get tough. The process of growth won't be easy; it will hurt, but don't quit. It's all part of the process to progress. Don't shy away from your potential. PUSH.

Keep your blinders on. Think of the horses in the major races, they have blinders on their eyes. They remain focused. They aren't distracted by their "competitors". Their only competition is their own personal best. They put all they have while staying in their lane. Their goal is to exceed their own personal best. There is no outside competition. Stay disciplined, persistent and focused. Keep your eye on the mission you've been uniquely assigned.

Part 3

Motivation

What pushes you daily? What are your strengths? What are your weaknesses? What are the things you do well? It's time to give your self-esteem the ultimate boost when you figure out what keeps you mentally motivated. What is your story? What are the things that you are most capable of doing? Identify them and heighten your value. Identify the sensitive areas of your life and seek help. When your self-esteem is built up, your motivation will be unstoppable.

What Makes You SPECIAL

I can

_____

_____

_____

_____

_____

_____

_____

_____

I have

_____

_____

_____

_____

_____

_____

_____

Telling People about Yourself

Imagine you are meeting someone for the first time.

Think of three things that you could tell them about yourself.

1.

_____

_____

2.

_____

_____

3.

_____

_____

PROMISES TO YOURSELF

I VOW TO . . .

Let my heart my heal

Be more confident

Work on maintaining healthy relationships

Discover my life's purpose

Move forward in all areas

Find peace

Reach my goals

Be content and happy

Go with the flow, and not live in frustration

Trust my intuition

Discover my authentic self

List your TOP ten accomplishments

1_____

2_____

3_____

4_____

5_____

6_____

7_____

8_____

9_____

10_____

I like myself because

_____

I do _____ very well

I feel good about _____

My friends would tell you I have a great _____

My favorite place is _____

_____ loves me

People say I am a good _____

I have been told that I have great _____

I consider myself a good _____

Like the way I feel about myself when I _____

What I really enjoy most is _____

The person I look up to the most is _____

The one person who always makes me feel good about
myself is

_____

I look good when _____

The color _____ looks great on me

I have a natural talent for _____

I am most happy when _____

My goals for the future are _____

One of the many positive traits I have is _____

People often compliment me about _____

My friends respect me because I always _____

I have a good sense of _____

The two things I do best are _____ and _____

I know that I will be successful in life because I will

_____

Life is like a game of cards, no matter how the deck is shuffled you are still ROYALTY.

30-Days to a Better you Challenge

~Start the Journey~

Day 1:

Be grateful

Make a list of the top ten Things you are grateful for. Reflect on this list throughout the day. An attitude of gratitude will brighten up your day

Daily Reflection:

_____

_____

_____

_____

_____

_____

_____

_____

_____

Day 2:

Goal getter

List your Top three goals for this month. Make a checklist of things you need to do to accomplish each goal. Pick a day each week to reassess each goal.

Daily Reflection:

_____

_____

_____

_____

_____

_____

_____

_____

Day 3:

Accept the past

Take some time to reflect on past regrets and disappointments. Write them on a sheet of paper. Now rip it up! Accept it and move forward.

Daily Reflection:

_____

_____

_____

_____

_____

_____

_____

_____

Day 4:

Be positive

Today, focus on being optimistic. Eliminate negative distractions and try to see the positive in every moment.

Daily Reflection:

_____

_____

_____

_____

_____

_____

_____

_____

Day 5:

Be social:

Smile. Be social. Network. Strike up a friendly conversation and show off your personality. This will brighten up your day.

Daily Reflection:

_____

_____

_____

_____

_____

_____

_____

_____

Day 6:

Don't rush:

Things happen in their own time. Be patient with the process of things. Oftentimes progress takes time.

Daily Reflection:

_____

_____

_____

_____

_____

_____

_____

_____

Day 7:

Release the stress:

Stress can be toxic for our bodies. Free your mind from stress with activities that will allow you to free yourself and to find release. Make a list of some things you can do soon to reduce your stress.

Daily Reflection:

_____

_____

_____

_____

_____

_____

_____

_____

_____

Day 8:

Get healthy:

The keys to being healthy include having good eating habits, exercising and staying hydrated. It's time to get active. Make a schedule today of what you can do to get healthy.

Daily Reflection:

_____

_____

_____

_____

_____

_____

_____

_____

Day 9:

Laugh it UP

Watch a funny video. Tell a joke. Read a comic strip. Do something today that will get your giggles going.

Daily Reflection:

_____

_____

_____

_____

_____

_____

_____

_____

Day 10:

Find your voice:

Speak up for yourself when the moment comes. Don't shy away from sharing your passions. Be bold and speak up today. With class and finesse of course!

Daily Reflection:

_____

_____

_____

_____

_____

_____

_____

_____

_____

Day 11:

Bless-UP

Count your blessings today! Say a quick prayer of thankfulness.

Daily Reflection:

_____

_____

_____

_____

_____

_____

_____

_____

Day 12:

Relax

Take five deep breathes. Do this again with your eyes closed. It may be time to schedule a massage

Daily Reflection:

_____

_____

_____

_____

_____

_____

_____

_____

_____

Day 13:

Be fearless

Be bold and fearless today. Seize the moment and be courageous.

Daily Reflection:

_____

_____

_____

_____

_____

_____

_____

_____

Day 14:

Pay it forward:

Do a random act of kindness today. Doing something kind for someone can go a long way.

Daily Reflection:

_____

_____

_____

_____

_____

_____

_____

_____

_____

Day 15:

Be pleasant:

Being nice seems to be a forgotten art. Aspire to have an attitude that is enjoyable. You get more bees with honey than vinegar.

Daily Reflection:

_____

_____

_____

_____

_____

_____

_____

_____

Day 16:

Refuel your faith

Take some time to reflect on your faith. Find some scriptures and quotes that will give your faith a boost.

Daily Reflection:

_____

_____

_____

_____

_____

_____

_____

_____

_____

Day 17:

Take a class

Think of a hobby that you've always wanted to develop. A cooking class would be a great example. Learn a new skill and expand your mind.

Daily Reflection:

_____

_____

_____

_____

_____

_____

_____

_____

_____

Day 18:

Call an old friend

Do you have an old friend you haven't heard from in a while? Reach out and catch up. It's always nice to reconnect.

Daily Reflection:

_____

_____

_____

_____

_____

_____

_____

_____

_____

Day 19:

Charity

There are so many people in the world who need help. Seek out these individuals and do God's work.

Daily Reflection:

_____

_____

_____

_____

_____

_____

_____

_____

Day 20:

Forgive

Make a list of individuals who need your forgiveness. Pray during this process. You may need courage to reach out to a few individuals.

Daily Reflection:

_____

_____

_____

_____

_____

_____

_____

_____

Day 21:

Be happy

Make a list of some of the happiest moments in your life. Now write down three new memories you would like to create.

Daily Reflection:

_____

_____

_____

_____

_____

_____

_____

_____

Day 22:

Affirmations

Refresh your affirmations. Write out your core values and create a personal mission statement.

Daily Reflection:

_____

_____

_____

_____

_____

_____

_____

_____

Day 23:

Share LOVE

Love is tangible. Show someone some love today. Whether through a text message or phone call, a hug or some freshly baked cookies. Share some love today.

Daily Reflection:

_____

_____

_____

_____

_____

_____

_____

_____

_____

Day 24:

Compliments count

When was the last time you gave someone a genuine compliment? Or do you remember the last time you gave yourself a compliment. Give yourself three compliments while looking in the mirror today. And find three persons to give genuine compliments to.

Daily Reflection:

_____

_____

_____

_____

_____

_____

_____

_____

Day 25:

Pray for peace

Life can be very hectic and filled with stress. Take some time to meditate and to pray for peace. Let go of the stress and receive God's peace.

Daily Reflection:

_____

_____

_____

_____

_____

_____

_____

_____

Day 26:

Into nature

Nature has a way of calming us. Make sure to go and spend some time at your local park, beach, or even a garden. Go appreciate the beauty of nature.

Daily Reflection:

_____

_____

_____

_____

_____

_____

_____

_____

_____

Day 27:

Hydrate!

Hydrate your body with water, and hydrate your soul with inspiring words.

Daily Reflection:

_____

_____

_____

_____

_____

_____

_____

_____

Day 28:

Be ambitious

There are some goal that you have been trying to achieve for years now. You need new motivations and a healthy dose of ambition. Find new ways to achieve some of your dreams. Go harder.

Daily Reflection:

_____

_____

_____

_____

_____

_____

_____

_____

_____

Day 29:

Have faith

There is power in your level of expectation! Stretch yourself and your faith in God.

Daily Reflection:

_____

_____

_____

_____

_____

_____

_____

_____

Day 30:

Journal

Take a moment and journal about the progress you've made over the past month. Take some time to reflect on the journey.

Daily Reflection:

_____

_____

_____

_____

_____

_____

_____

_____

EPILOGUE

The purpose of this book is to remind you that you are not a fraction. You are a whole person. You were created on purpose, for a specific purpose. Negative perceptions corrupt our thoughts and sabotage our destiny. Don't let them corrode you self-worth.
Life is defined by the standards, principles and core beliefs that govern our actions. As we move through life, outside factors may shape the way we perceive ourselves. But when we realize the worth we have because we were created by God, we can walk in our worth and achieve even the impossible,
In order to live your best life:
Activate your potential
Discipline your laziness
Reset your setbacks
Upgrade your standard
Walk in your purpose

Live your worth!
—Daniela

Share your Thoughts ❧

_____

_____

_____

_____

_____

_____

_____

_____

_____

_____

_____

_____

_____

_____

_____

_____

_____

_____

_____

_____

_____

_____

_____

Share your Thoughts ❧

Share your Thoughts ❧

_____

_____

_____

_____

_____

_____

_____

_____

_____

_____

_____

_____

_____

_____

_____

_____

_____

_____

_____

_____

Connect with me on:
Instagram|Facebook| Twitter| YouTube
@DaniEmpowers

Made in the USA
Middletown, DE
11 March 2022